Discovering

SPIDERS

Malcolm Penny

The Bookwright Press
New York · 1986

Discovering Nature

Discovering Bees and Wasps
Discovering Snakes and Lizards
Discovering Spiders
Discovering Worms

Further titles are in preparation

All photographs from Oxford Scientific Films

First published in the United States in 1986 by
The Bookwright Press
387 Park Avenue South
New York, NY 10016

First published in 1985 by
Wayland (Publishers) Limited
61 Western Road, Hove
East Sussex BN3 1JD, England

© Copyright 1985 Wayland (Publishers) Limited

Second impression 1986

ISBN 0-531-18045-X
Library of Congress Catalog Card Number: 85-62088

Typeset by Planagraphic Typesetters Limited
Printed in Italy by G. Canale & C.S.p.A., Turin

Contents

Introducing Spiders

Spiders Everywhere

Over 30,000 different spiders have been found in the world, and more are being discovered every day. There are more than 3,000 different kinds in Europe alone, though some of them are very rare.

The American tarantula is one of the world's biggest spiders.

Spiders can live almost anywhere, from the seashore to the tops of mountains. One type of spider lives nearly 7,000 meters (23,000 feet) up on Mount Everest, and others are found in deep caves and coal mines. There is only one which lives permanently underwater, though others hunt in ponds, on beaches, and even on coral reefs. In fact wherever any other small animal can live, there will be a spider to hunt it.

The biggest spider ever discovered is the bird spider in South America. It eats small lizards and large insects. One had a body 10 cm (4 inches) long, and legs 25 cm (10 inches) across.

The smallest spider ever found lives among moss on the Pacific island of Samoa. It is less than half a millimeter long when it is fully grown. You need a microscope to see that it is a spider.

Few spiders have names in English. Most people who study them use their Latin names, but in this book we have translated the Latin into a made-up

Garden spiders are found all over the world. This one is making a web.

name in English. Made-up names are in inverted commas followed by the Latin name in brackets, like this: 'sulking spider' *(Dysdera)*. A name without inverted commas, like garden spider, is the usual English language name.

A Spider's Body

A spider has two main parts to its body, the **head-and-thorax,** and the **abdomen.** The abdomen is joined to the head-and-thorax by a narrow waist. Attached to the head-and-thorax are four pairs of jointed legs, and one pair each of jaws and

Below *An orb-weaving spider with its cast-off skeleton hanging above it.*

Above *You can see the silk coming out of this garden spider's spinnerets.*

palps. Each jaw is tipped with a sharp **fang,** through which poison can be pumped into the spider's **prey.** The palps of a male spider have swellings which are used in mating, but those of a female are slender.

A spider's legs, jaws, palps and fangs are hollow and are controlled by muscles from the inside. This arrangement is called an external skeleton. As it grows, the spider casts off its external skeleton, and stretches the new one, which has formed underneath, before it hardens. This casting-off is called **molting.** One advantage of molting is that the spider can regrow and replace any lost limbs.

On top and in front of a spider's head are four, or sometimes six, pairs of eyes.

At the tip of the abdomen is a group of six **spinnerets.** These are nozzles through which the spider pumps out liquid silk. Under the front end of the abdomen, two pale patches mark the position of the **lung-books,** by which the spider breathes. Near the slits that lead to the lung-books is the opening to the sex organs.

The Parts of a Spider's Body

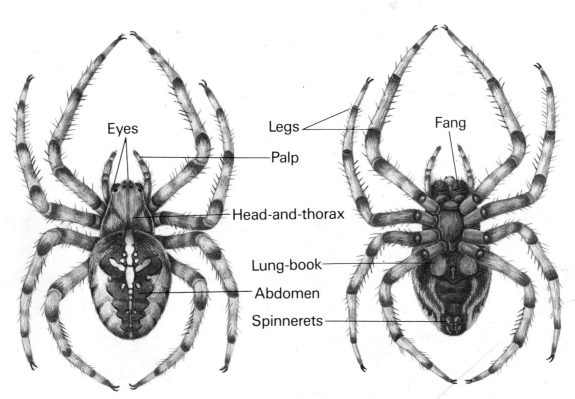

Eyes
Legs
Fang
Palp
Head-and-thorax
Lung-book
Abdomen
Spinnerets

11

Where Spiders Live

Spiders Around the World

Some spiders, like house spiders and garden spiders, can be found all over the world.

House spiders make large webs in moist, dark rooms. The webs of one type of house spider were once used for dressing wounds. Some kinds of house spider also live in quarries and forests.

Garden spiders weave **orb-webs.** This is a common type of web. Some garden spiders make a retreat in a rolled up leaf near the web. You can find garden spiders in parks, gardens and wooded areas.

Below *Many people are frightened when they see a long-legged house spider in their home, but they are harmless.*

Nursery web spiders live and hunt in grass and among other plants. Some nursery web spiders can run across water to catch their prey. They are called raft, or fishing, spiders.

As its name suggests, a daddy-longlegs has very long legs. Most kinds of daddy-longlegs make loose webs in dark corners in houses and in cellars. Other types live under stones and on low vegetation.

Above *Raft spiders sometimes reach below the surface of the water to catch prey.*

Below *Daddy-longlegs like dark places and are often found in houses.*

Some other spiders that are found all over the world are jumping spiders, crab spiders, nursery web spiders and daddy-longlegs. Most crab spiders and jumping spiders live in tropical countries, but many kinds are found in North America and Europe. Some tropical giant crab spiders have been brought into cooler countries in boxes of bananas, but they cannot live long in the cold.

In Cool Lands

The cool climate of Britain, Canada and the northern parts of Europe and the U.S. is favorable for many kinds of spiders.

The majority of spiders in the Arctic and on high mountains are wolf spiders. Most wolf spiders hunt their prey on the ground. One type, the pirate wolf spider,

Below *A pirate wolf spider carrying her egg-sac across the water's surface.*

lives by the water and hunts over the surface of ponds and marshes.

Dwarf spiders are usually found in cool European countries and North America. Many live in the Arctic and on high mountains. Dwarf spiders live under stones, in fallen leaves and in the grass.

The only true water spider is found in ponds and streams in Britain, other European countries and in some parts of Asia. It lives underwater in a bubble of air which it traps in its bell-shaped web.

Above *The water spider is the only spider which can swim freely underwater.*

Water spiders **hibernate** in the winter.

Other spiders commonly found in cool climates are the funnel weaver spider, which makes a flat web in the grass or in low bushes; the purseweb spider which digs a hole in the ground and lays a hidden silken trap above its hole; and many different orb-weaving spiders which make webs, like those of the garden spider.

15

In Hot Lands

Some of the largest and most colorful spiders live in hot countries — in the jungles and deserts of South America, Africa, the southern United States, the Caribbean, Asia and Australia.

Most crab spiders, like this one from Trinidad, have well-developed front legs with which to grab insects.

Most crab spiders are found in the tropics. Some are the same color as the flowers they live in; others look like birds' droppings and live in plants.

The huntsman spider is a giant crab spider. It often lives in houses, where it is welcome because it eats cockroaches.

The six-eyed crab spider lives in dry, sandy parts of South America and Africa. It can disappear completely by digging itself into the sand.

All jumping spiders are small and most of them live in warm countries. Jumping spiders can be found on the ground and on plants and trees. Some types of jumping spiders look like ants, which protects them from predators.

There are many poisonous spiders in warm countries, like the brown recluse which is found in South America and south eastern parts of the United States; the black widow spider which is found in most warm parts of the world; and the deadly Australian funnelweb spider.

Most trapdoor spiders are tropical,

Above *Jumping spiders have one pair of eyes much larger than the others.*

Right *A trapdoor spider coming out of its silk-lined tunnel.*

though some are found in southern parts of the United States and Europe. They live underground in tube-like burrows.

Tarantulas are large and hairy but most of them are harmless. Many people keep tarantulas as pets.

Webs and Other Traps

Building a Web

There are almost as many different kinds of webs as there are types of web-building spiders. The most familiar is the vertical orb-web of the garden spider. It is fascinating to watch an orb-web being built, most often by a female. Adult males do not build webs. First, the spider makes a bridge by letting out a fine strand of silk until it touches a suitable point of attachment. Having strengthened this first thread, she spins another to hang loosely below it. She then drops vertically from the middle of this loop until she finds an anchoring place. She has now made a Y-shaped framework, with the top points joined. These are the first three spokes of her web. She then spins other threads which meet at the center of the Y until the framework is complete.

After making a small spiral at the center to lock the spokes in position, she spins a temporary spiral from the center to the edge of the web. She then works her way back to the center, taking up the temporary spiral and laying a sticky spiral in its place. The web is now ready to catch flying insects. To prevent themselves from being stuck to their own glue, spiders that build sticky webs produce an oily substance with which they cover their legs.

Right *A garden spider making an orb-web.*
Below *One of the many kinds of orb-weaving spider is the green cucumber spider.*

18

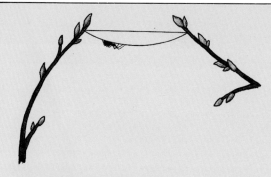

1. *Making the bridge line*

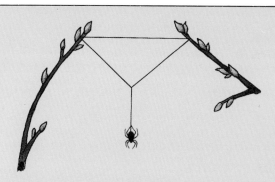

2. *Y-shaped framework*

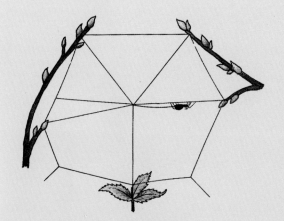

3. *Framework complete*

4. *Making central spiral to lock spokes*

5. *Finishing temporary, non-sticky spiral*

6. *Permanent sticky web nearly finished*

Webs as Traps

Some spiders build webs that are not sticky, but made of fluffy silk, in which the victim's claws and bristles become entangled. The lace-web, or featherlegged, spider makes an orb-web very like that of the garden spider, but horizontal rather than vertical. The final spiral is made of silk which she has fluffed out with combs on her back legs. Unlike most spiders, the

The silk spun by the lace-web spider is fluffed out to entangle prey.

lace-web spider has no poison glands, so her first act on catching an insect is to wrap it with more silk before it escapes.

A much more common spider, whose web is not sticky, is the sheet-web spider. Her trap is a horizontal sheet of woven silk, usually among grass, with a funnel near the middle in which the spider waits for prey to arrive. Above the sheet is a messy tangle of threads. Grasshoppers often fall into this trap, being stopped in mid-hop by the loose threads, and falling down among the tighter ones until they are hopelessly tangled. When they reach the sheet, the spider can approach and bite her victims at leisure, before dragging them back to the funnel to eat.

Higher up in bushes and shrubs, the tiny money spiders make similar traps in which they catch flying insects, especially greenflies.

Right *The morning dew has covered the scaffolding and catching platform of a sheet-web spider's web.*

21

Sticky Snares

When a garden spider, a type of orb-weaving spider, catches an insect, she wraps it quickly in bands of non-sticky silk, before killing it with her poisonous bite. Not all spiders that make sticky webs use them in the same way.

Some of the little comb-footed spiders make webs that look very disorganized, like tangled scaffolding. The web reaches from the lair down to the ground, a matter of a few centimeters. This snare traps crawling insects, often ants. The strands of silk that reach the ground have a few drops of glue at the bottom. When an ant touches one, the spider pulls

Below *An orb-weaver spider with its wrapped-up prey.*

Above *A black widow spider has to carefully wrap up a scorpion before eating it.*

it up, leaving the ant dangling in mid-air. The spider then wraps its prey in sticky silk, using the combs on its back feet, from which the group gets its name.

The famous black widow is a comb-footed spider. She uses a similar trap to catch quite large prey, including scorpions. Other comb-footed spiders spread their glue around the middle of their webs to catch insects in flight.

Moths can often escape from sticky webs. This is because they have loose scales on their wings which stick to the glue, giving them a chance to fly away.

This untidy web was made by a comb-footed spider. Its lair is at the top of its sticky trap.

A 'mantle spider' at the entrance to its burrow.

Trapdoor spiders use their jaws to dig burrows 30 cm (12 inches) or more long.

Tunnels and Trapdoors

The common 'mantle spider' (Segestria) lives in a burrow. It surrounds the entrance of its burrow with strands of white silk. Each strand is a trip-wire, alerting the spider when a crawling insect passes near the hole. It can then rush out and drag the prey into its burrow to eat.

In warmer countries, trapdoor spiders set a more complicated ambush. They too have trip-wires, but the entrance to the hole has a hinged lid. When a victim comes within range, the spider opens the lid suddenly, grabs its prey, and pulls it underground.

In cooler countries, the purseweb spider lays a similar trap. It lives in a sealed tube of silk, most of which is underground. The upper part of the European purseweb spider's tube, about 2.5 cm (1 inch) long, lies on the ground, hidden with grains of soil. The American purseweb spider makes its burrow at the base of a tree. It then builds its silken trap up the side of the tree.

The purseweb spider waits inside its burrow for an unsuspecting insect to walk across its trap. Then the spider strikes upward with both fangs, piercing the silk tube and its prey. It then cuts a hole in the tube and drags the victim inside. After catching its prey the spider always repairs its purse with new silk.

__Above__ The American purseweb spider's trap can extend as much as 15 cm (6 inches) up the side of a tree. __Below__ The European purseweb spider's trap is usually 22 cm (9 inches) long. Purseweb spiders can grow to 30 mm (1 inch) long.

1. A purseweb spider seen inside its burrow.

2. The spider has pierced through its web to catch a fly.

Spiders as Hunters

Unusual Hunters

Some spiders catch their prey in very unusual ways. The net-casting spider hunts by night in woodlands and gardens. The spider hangs by its front legs from a few strands of silk and weaves a small web of fluffy silk with its back legs. When it has finished, it passes the web to its front four legs and hangs head downwards, holding the web close to the ground. It watches until a small insect passes underneath, and then quickly places the web over it. Picking the web up, it shakes it until the prey is well and truly entangled. The spider then eats its victim and web together.

Another very odd hunter is called the magnificent, or bolas, spider. It hangs from a bush and swings a strand of silk, with a blob of glue at the end, with one front leg. Because the glue smells like a

A net-casting spider ready to pounce on the next insect that walks under its trap.

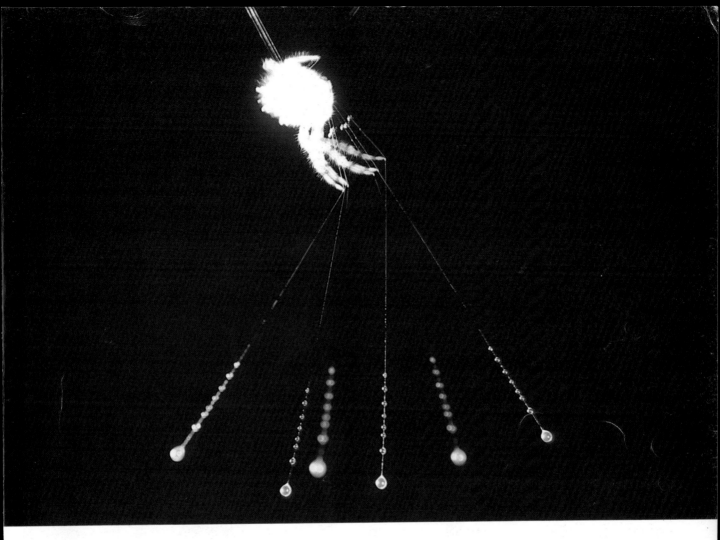

The bolas spider uses a silken thread, armed with a drop of glue, to catch prey.

female moth, male moths fly towards it. The silken lasso sticks to one of the moths, and the spider hauls it up to eat.

Another unusual spider is called the spitting spider. It can squirt a jet of gum from each fang, to stick its victim down until it can kill it with a bite. It then drags its prey free of the sticky patch, and takes it away to eat.

Hunting and Stalking

Wolf spiders are great hunters. They are common in woodland, meadows, marshes, and even on the seashore. They do not spin webs, but with good eyesight and long legs, they catch their prey by chasing it. Most wolf spiders are only half a centimeter (quarter of an inch) long, but they are fierce and successful predators on small insects.

A very different hunter is the 'sulking spider' *(Dysdera)*. It is stout and slow-moving, but it can catch woodlice. Most spiders will not eat woodlice because of their heavy armor and evil taste, but the sulking spider's long fangs can penetrate the body easily. The unpleasant chemical which the woodlouse produces to defend

Below *Hunting wolf spiders may look fierce, but most of them are harmless.*

itself does not affect the spider, because its long fangs kill the woodlouse before it comes too close to the spider's face.

Some of the most active and attractive spiders are the jumping spiders, which stalk their prey like tiny cats. They have large eyes, especially the middle pair, and powerful legs. Their feet have sticky pads, to give them a good grip. A jumping spider will creep slowly towards a fly until it is about a centimeter (half an inch) away, and then spring forward to seize it with its front legs and fangs. In case it should fall, a jumping spider trails a lifeline of silk wherever it goes.

Above *Jumping spiders use strands of silk as life-lines just as mountaineers use ropes.*

Below *A 'sulking spider' piercing the armor of a woodlouse.*

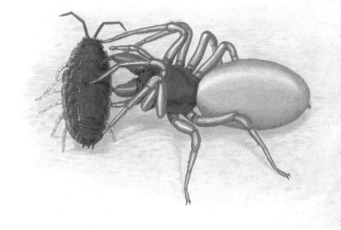

Camouflaged Spiders

Many animals, including spiders, must hide from other animals which would eat them if they could find them. Some spiders hide by day and hunt only at night, but others are protected by being **camouflaged** with colors and patterns which match their background. Many spiders that live in a cool climate are brownish or grayish in color, to match the soil or dead leaves, though most spiders have a patterned abdomen.

30

You have to look very carefully to see this camouflaged wolf spider.

Some tropical spiders are camouflaged with much brighter colors, particularly those that hunt among flowers. The beautiful crab spiders match the flowers in which they live so exactly that when they stand still they are almost invisible. There are many different kinds of crab spiders living all over the world. They are so called because they hold their front legs out sideways like crabs. They can also walk sideways. Some crab spiders change color, slowly, when they move to a different flower.

Crab spiders are camouflaged not only to escape from their enemies, but also to help catch their prey. Sitting without moving on a flower, a crab spider is invisible to butterflies as well as to birds, which might eat it. When a butterfly lands to feed at the flower, the spider seizes it with its front legs and bites to kill.

Not all brightly colored spiders are trying to hide. Some, especially the more poisonous ones, often with red or yellow on a black background, are warning their enemies to keep away.

A pink crab spider hides inside a foxglove. It grabs insects that visit the flower.

Survival in a Dangerous World

Enemies of Spiders

Humans are not the worst enemy of spiders, except perhaps in some people's houses. A very serious enemy is the weather, especially in uncertain climates. A female spider has only a short breeding season in which to collect enough food to develop her eggs. In cooler countries there may not be enough fine days for her to collect as much food as she needs to keep even herself alive.

More obvious enemies are frogs and toads, lizards, and birds. Spiders are also important food for small woodland mammals, such as shrews, which hunt endlessly among leaves and grass. Hunting beetles, ants, and centipedes also kill a great many spiders.

Among the spider's most dangerous enemies are parasitic flies and wasps. Some hunting wasps seek out wolf spiders, even though the spider might be bigger than the wasp itself, and sting them so that they cannot move. Then the wasp digs a burrow in the ground, and buries the spider after laying an egg on it. When the egg hatches, the wasp grub eats the paralyzed spider alive.

Tiger beetles move fast and can easily catch and kill spiders with their big jaws.

Above *Some hunting wasps attack spiders which are more than twice their size.*

There is even a fungus which kills spiders by growing in their bodies. However, because most small hunting animals are spiders, the greatest enemy, especially of young spiders, is other spiders.

When this wasp egg hatches, the grub will eat the paralyzed tarantula.

The amount of red on a black widow spider varies from country to country.

Deadly to Humans

Almost all spiders use **venom** to kill and to help digest their prey, but very few of them can harm humans. Few northern European spiders are harmful, though

some of the biggest ones might bite you if you picked them up.

Of all the spiders that have killed people, the most famous is the European tarantula. Many years ago, in the town of Taranto in Italy, people who were bitten by spiders became ill, and some died. It was believed that the only way of saving them was to make them dance until they

34

dropped. The dance was called the Tarantella. Tarantulas are still common around the town of Taranto, from which they get their name.

However, the real villain was a smaller spider with a much worse bite, called the black widow. These shiny black spiders with red markings are found in warm countries, from America to New Zealand. They are known by a variety of names such as "redback" or "button spider." The bite seldom kills a healthy adult, but children and old people have died from it. The American tarantula is a large hairy spider, as big as a hand, which looks very frightening but is completely harmless.

Another spider, found in America and Australia, with a most unpleasant bite, is the brown recluse. It very rarely kills people, but the wound it leaves may take over a year to heal.

The venom of the brown recluse spider causes ulcers that take months to heal.

Reproduction

Above *The smaller of these two courting house spiders is the male.*

Right *The paler of these two courting tarantulas is the female.*

Courtship and Mating

A male spider prepares for mating, as soon as he is fully grown, by spinning a minute web. He deposits drops of **sperm** on the web which he then sucks into each palp in turn. Then he goes in search of a female. His main problem in courting is to convince the female that he is not something to eat.

Web-builders, like the garden spider, court a female by twanging the strands of

Above *If you look carefully, you can see a tiny male on the belly of this female orb-weaving spider.*

her web. When she attacks, the male drops out of the web on a safety line. He repeats his efforts until she comes to hang beside him on his special mating thread.

A male wolf spider walks very slowly towards a female, signaling to her with movements of his palps, or his legs, or both. When she vibrates her legs in response, mating can begin.

A male nursery web spider presents the female with a fly wrapped in silk. He mates with her while she is busy feeding.

All spiders mate in much the same way. The male inserts his palps, loaded with sperm, one at a time into the female's sexual opening. The sperm passes into her, to be stored within her body until she is ready to lay her eggs.

Laying Eggs

All spiders lay eggs in a similar way. The female spins a saucer-shaped disk of silk, firmly attached to a support such as a blade of grass or a wall. Crouching over it, she then produces the eggs, together

An orb-weaving spider laying eggs on her cushion of silk.

with a blob of liquid which holds them together like the seeds in a tomato. The eggs settle into the middle of the saucer.

The female then spins more silk as a

lid over the saucer to seal the edge. The resulting pie-shaped object is called an **egg-sac.** The smallest spiders lay only two eggs at a time, but a well-fed garden spider can lay as many as a thousand.

Some species leave the egg-sac where it was made, but most remove it and spin more silk around it to form a ball. Some then hang the ball in the web. Others carry it round with them until the eggs are ready to hatch. Wolf spiders carry the ball hanging from their spinnerets and nursery web spiders grip it with their jaws as well. Daddy-longlegs carry theirs in their jaws alone.

After two to four weeks, some females loosen the outer strands of the egg-sac, ready for their babies to emerge. Eggs laid late in the autumn may hatch as late as the following spring.

Right *The fluffy outer layer of the nursery web spider's egg-sac hardens and has to be unpicked before the baby spiders can emerge.*

Above *The female spider covers her eggs with spun silk to make an egg-sac.*

Baby Spiders

Newly-hatched baby spiders are blind and helpless, unable to feed or to spin silk.

They are not ready to come out from the egg-sac until after their second molt.

Some cut their way out as soon as they are ready, often with their mother's help, but others stay inside the egg-sac until the weather is suitable for them to come out. Some, like young garden spiders, clump together when they emerge. Baby wolf spiders climb onto their mother's back.

Eventually, they will all need to feed. Some of the comb-footed spiders have food brought to them by their mother. Others make their own webs, to catch tiny flying or hopping insects. Baby spiders must soon move apart because there is danger that they might eat each other.

Although many young spiders simply walk away, others travel by air. They spin a long strand of fine silk by which the breeze lifts them off the ground. The

Left *Baby wolf spiders are carried on their mother's back.*

dangers of traveling like this are many: they might land where there is no food to be found, or they might be eaten in mid-air by a bird. Huge numbers of baby spiders die at this stage, but some eventually land in places which are suitable for them to live.

Baby nursery web spiders live for a few days inside a silken tent made by their mother.

Learning About Spiders

In Parks and Gardens

You can recognize most spiders by their webs. To see the spider itself, you might have to be patient. The garden spider's web is easy to recognize, but what does a garden spider eat? You will find the bodies of her victims on the ground below the web. If you unwrap the silk parcels carefully, with two pins, you will discover what she has been catching.

Below *A garden spider wrapping a fly in silk before eating it.*

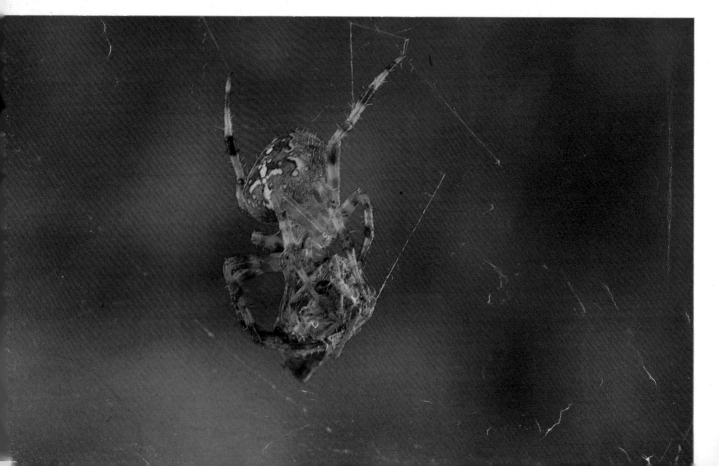

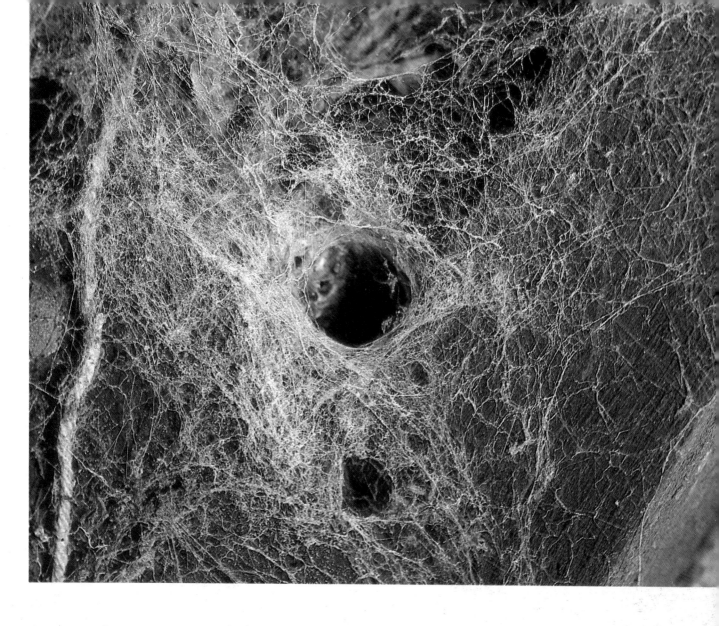

Above *The entrance to a 'darkling spider's' burrow is surrounded by a white collar made of many strands of silk.*

Look for a silk collar around a hole in a wall, surrounded by straight trip-wires. Touch one gently with a blade of grass, and be ready for a mantle spider to dart out. If there are no trip wires, a 'darkling spider' (*Amaurobius*) will come out when you touch the silk collar.

To look closely at money spiders and lace-web spiders you will have to catch them in a small jam-jar, and use a magnifying glass. Put a blade of grass in the jar for the spider to stand on. The Zebra spider, a kind of jumping spider, is hard

The face of a garden spider seen under a magnifying glass.

The zebra spider, a kind of jumping spider, is easiest to find on sunny walls.

to catch, but very beautiful to look at. Notice how it moves its head-and-thorax to watch you.

When you have had a close look at a spider, and perhaps drawn a picture of it, you should let it go. Open the jar close to the spider's web, and let it walk out. Never shake the jar, or you might damage the spider.

Glossary

Abdomen The rear part of a spider's body, which contains the stomach.

Camouflage The color, pattern, or shape by which an animal matches its background and is therefore hidden.

Egg-sac The silk container in which spiders protect their eggs.

Fang The sharp spike with which the spider bites its prey and injects venom.

Head-and-thorax The front part of a spider's body. Another name for it is cephalothorax.

Hibernate To spend the winter sleeping.

Lung-book The chamber in a spider's abdomen by which it breathes.

Molting The process of casting off a skin which an animal has outgrown, to reveal a new one underneath.

Orb-web A round flat web with spokes, like that of the garden spider.

Palp One of two feelers beside a spider's jaws, with which it tastes its surroundings.

Prey An animal that is killed and eaten by another animal.

Sperm The cells produced by a male which fertilize a female's eggs.

Spinneret One of six nozzles at the tip of a spider's abdomen. They produce silk.

Venom A liquid which kills or paralyzes prey.

Finding Out More

If you would like to find out more about spiders, you could read the following books:

Dallinger, Jane. *Spiders.* Minneapolis, MN: Lerner Publications, 1981.

Levi, Herbert and Levi, Lorna. *Spiders and Their Kin.* New York: Western, 1979.

Podendorf, Ila. *Spiders.* Chicago: Childrens Press, 1982.

Ryder, Joanne. *The Spiders Dance.* New York: Harper & Row, 1981.

Victor, Joan B. *Tarantulas.* New York: Dodd, Mead, 1979.

Walther, Tom. *A Spider Might.* New York: Charles Scribner, 1978.

Index

Picture Acknowledgments

All photographs from Oxford Scientific Films by the following photographers: G. I. Bernard 14, 18, 41; J. A. L. Cooke cover, 9, 10 (top), 13, 15, 16, 17, 20, 21, 23 (right), 24 (left), 26, 28, 33 (bottom), 34, 35, 36, 38, 39, 42, 44 (top); S. Dalton opp. title page, 22, 29; M. Fogden 33 (top); Mantis Wildlife Films 27; S. R. Morris 10 (bottom), 24 (right), 31, 37; K. Porter 40; A. Ramage 13, 23 (left); P. K. Sharpe 8, 32; G. H. Thompson 30; P. & W. Ward 12; B. E. Watts 43, 44 (bottom). Artwork by Wendy Meadway.